Quilled Borders & Motifs

JUDY CARDINAL

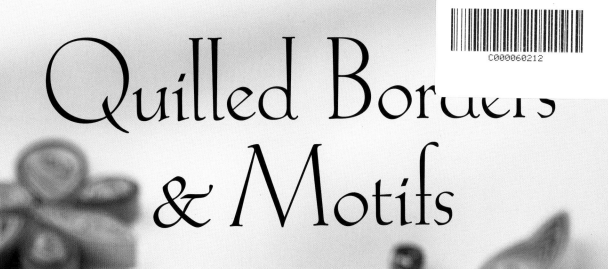

SEARCH PRESS

First published in Great Britain 2008

Search Press Limited
Wellwood, North Farm Road,
Tunbridge Wells, Kent TN2 3DR

Text copyright © Judy Cardinal 2008

Photographs by Roddy Paine Photographic Studio

Photographs and design copyright © Search Press Ltd. 2008

ISBN 13: 978-1-84448-208-5

The Publishers and author can accept no responsibility for
any consequences arising from the information, advice or
instructions given in this publication.

Readers are permitted to reproduce any of the items in this
book for their personal use, or for the purposes of selling
for charity, free of charge and without the prior permission
of the Publishers. Any use of the items for commercial
purposes is not permitted without the prior permission of the
Publishers.

Suppliers
If you have difficulty in obtaining any of the materials and
equipment mentioned in this book, then please visit the
Search Press website for details of suppliers:
www.searchpress.com

Dedication
To Joan for all the fun we had.

Acknowledgements
I would like to thank all my crafting friends for
their support, especially those in my quilling
classes who were forever asking me to put all
my ideas down in a book. My thanks also go
to Search Press for allowing this dream to be
fulfilled, especially to Katie, my editor, who
guided me through. Lastly, thank you to my
long-suffering husband and family who put
up with months of 'sorry I have to work on the
book!' and who have supported me throughout.

Publishers' note

All the step-by-step photographs in this book feature
the author, Judy Cardinal, demonstrating quilling. No
models have been used.

Conversion table

Throughout this book, strip lengths are given as
fractions of a full-length strip, as detailed below:

1 strip = 450mm (18in)
$\frac{1}{2}$ strip = 225mm (9in)
$\frac{1}{3}$ strip = 150mm (6in)
$\frac{1}{4}$ strip = 112mm (4½in)
$\frac{1}{8}$ strip = 56mm (2¼in)
$\frac{1}{16}$ strip = 28mm (1¼in)

Mark your quilling board with these lengths as a quick
reference. It is not necessary to measure each strip
– simply fold the strip into half, quarter, etc. and cut.

Contents

All of the designs on these two pages can be made from the basic quilled shapes described on pages 10–17.

Introduction

I have always loved playing with colour and design, but sadly drawing and painting are not my forte. Quilling is therefore wonderful for me, as the range of colours and different types of paper available allow me to be really creative without the need to draw. I very rarely create the same design twice – a very different look can often be achieved by simply varying the size or the colours used. I hope, through this book, to encourage you to experiment and change your designs so that everything you create is your own unique piece of work.

It is not necessary to keep to the colours and forms found in nature – a floral motif in shades of white and blue can be very effective. Try red frogs for fun, or bright, clashing colours on an abstract bird or fish. Quilling can take your imagination anywhere you like, and nothing is wrong if it pleases you.

There are clear instructions at the beginning of the book on the materials and equipment you need to get started; the basic techniques involved; how to create a quilled motif; and how to arrange your borders and motifs on greetings cards, picture frames, gift boxes and so on. In the remainder of the book I have provided a variety of designs which I hope will excite and inspire you, giving you a source of ideas for your own quilling projects.

All the borders and motifs shown here, and on pages 24–43, are actual size, and have been made using 3mm ($\frac{1}{8}$in) wide paper strips; instructions for most are provided, apart from the simpler ones which I feel are self-explanatory. Templates for the more intricate designs are provided on pages 44–47.

Materials and equipment

Quilling is a creative but inexpensive craft requiring a basic starter kit of only quilling papers, a quilling tool, glue and card. As you progress, there are many beautiful papers to collect to add variety to your work, plus some extra pieces of equipment which can be useful.

Quilling papers

Quilling papers come in many colours, from delicate pastels to vibrant darker shades. Packs of papers are available in rainbow mixes, shades of the same colour or single colours. It is helpful as a beginner to start with a rainbow-mix pack of papers and progress to the shaded and single colours when you have developed your own style of quilling and know which colours you enjoy working with.

Papers come in a variety of widths, from 1mm (¹⁄₂₄in) up to 10mm (½in) wide. The usual width used is 3mm (⅛in) and this will be used throughout this book.

Instructions in this book are given as fractions of a basic 450mm (18in) strip (please refer to the conversion table on page 2).

Graduated papers

Graduated papers are very pale at each end of the strip and get progressively darker towards the centre. When coiled, they give a shaded effect to the quilled shapes, as illustrated on the daisy leaves below.

Metallic- and pearl-edged papers

Papers are available with a gold, silver or other metallic finish to the edge of the strip, and also with delicate, pearlescent edges. These papers come in a variety of colours and are particularly effective for Christmas quilling designs or for special celebrations such as weddings and anniversaries.

Card blanks, papers and card

Many colours and sizes of ready-scored blank cards can be bought from craft shops, or alternatively you can fold and score your own cards from sheets of cardstock. Quilling is enhanced if it is mounted on backing papers or on a card shape whose colour tones with that of the base card. It is helpful to have a good variety of colours to try the quilled shapes on before gluing down. It is not always the first combination of colours you try that is the most effective – be prepared to experiment.

Picture frames and gift boxes

Gift boxes come in many shapes and sizes and can make a gift really special if they are personalised by adding a quilled motif to the lid or the sides of the box. Many of the quilled borders in this book can be used around picture frames or mounts. These can be very effective if the quilling reflects the colours and subject of the photograph.

Quilling tools and equipment

There are several varieties of quilling tool on the market. I find the easiest to use are the wooden-handled tools with a fine-slot needle. These give a tight centre to the quilled shapes and are comfortable to use. Plastic and metal tools are also available.

Good quality PVA glue is the best adhesive to use as it dries clear. It can be applied with a cocktail stick or a fine-tip glue applicator.

A quilling board of cork or fibreboard (or any board into which you can stick pins) should be used to assemble your design. Take care to avoid gluing your work to the board, and place a piece of white paper on the board first to keep it clean. If you are using a template, protect it with a sheet of greaseproof or tracing paper.

A selection of short and long round-headed pins and dressmaking pins is useful for holding the different parts of your motif in place as you assemble it. You will also need a small, sharp pair of scissors, a round-ended knife to loosen any quilled shapes that may get stuck to the board, a pair of tweezers for manipulating small pieces of quilling, and a hole punch for making holes in gift tags, etc.

Embellishments

Optional embellishments for quilled designs are ribbons, pearl or seed beads, joggle eyes and stickers. The easiest way to attach beads to your work is to place a dot of glue where it is needed using a cocktail stick, and then drop the bead on to the glue.

Basic quilling techniques

The craft of quilling essentially involves coiling narrow strips of paper to form intricate shapes and patterns. Most shapes are formed from a basic closed coil. There are also more advanced quilling techniques, such as filigree quilling where the shapes are not glued closed, quilled roses and wheatears (single looping). These are all described on the following eight pages.

Basic closed coil

The size of the basic closed coil is varied by using different lengths of quilling paper. When coiling, wind the tool either towards you or away from you, whichever comes naturally.

1 Insert the end of the paper strip into the slot at the end of the quilling tool.

2 Start to turn the quilling tool so that the paper winds tightly around it.

Tip

While coiling, cover the end of the tool with the index finger of your other hand to stop the paper coil slipping off, and hold the paper firmly between your thumb and third finger to maintain tension.

3 When you come to the end of the strip, loosen the coil slightly and remove the quilling tool, allowing the coil to unwind like a spring.

4 Put a small dab of PVA glue on the end of the paper to seal the coil. Make sure you spread the glue right to the edge of the paper.

5 Seal the coil by pressing down lightly on the join with your finger.

Shapes

Starting with the basic closed coil, various shapes can be formed by simply pinching and shaping it with the fingers.

A basic closed coil.

Teardrop

Pinch the basic closed coil at one end using your thumb and forefinger.

Leaf

Pinch the basic closed coil at both ends and twist.

Triangle

Form the coil into a triangle using three fingers, then pinch out one corner and flatten the other side.

Bell

Hold the basic closed coil with both hands, slide your forefingers down to form the sides, then pinch out the two corners at the base of the bell.

Square

Squeeze the basic closed coil between the thumb and forefinger of each hand to form an even-sided diamond.

Holly leaf

Pinch both sides of the closed coil and then push the fingers together to form two more points.

Marquise

Pinch out the basic closed coil at both ends to form a long, thin shape.

Half moon

Pinch out each end, as you did for the marquise, then curl the shape into a crescent moon.

The basic shapes used in this book, all derived from the basic closed coil.

Peg

The peg is the only shape to be glued tightly while it is still on the quilling tool. A peg is often used to form flower centres or for candles on Christmas cards.

1 Form a basic closed coil, as shown on page 10.

2 Glue down the end of the paper while it is still wound tightly on the quilling tool.

3 Carefully remove the quilling tool, twisting it slightly as you do so to help loosen it.

4 Lay the peg on a flat surface, and flatten it with the end of the quilling tool.

The completed peg.

Each 'eye' on this beautiful peacock is a peg made from a ⅛ black strip, a ⅛ deep blue strip, a ¼ gold-edged white strip and a ¼ jade green strip joined together in series, then coiled starting with the black. The seven tail feathers are wheatears (see page 16), and the body is a tightly coiled teardrop made from two blue and two turquoise strips joined in parallel. The head is also a teardrop, made from a blue ½ strip and a turquoise ½ strip joined in parallel with a hole left in the centre for the eye, which is a loose peg shape squeezed into an oval made from a white ⅛ strip and a black ⅛ strip joined in series. The two feet are ¼ strip indented triangles and the head feathers are three ⅛ strips coiled down part of their length. (See template on page 44.)

Joining two strips

Two or more strips joined in series (end to end) can be used to make a peg of two or more colours, as seen in the feathers of the peacock on page 12. This is also a very effective way to introduce colour variation within a flower petal or leaf. Two strips joined in parallel (one on top of the other) gives a multicoloured effect to a coil. Use two shades of the same colour for a more subtle effect, or two contrasting colours for impact.

Joining two strips in parallel

1 Apply glue to the end of one strip.

2 Glue the two strips together, one on top of the other.

Joining two strips in series

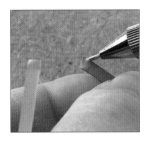

1 Apply glue to the end of one strip.

2 Lay the glued end on top of the end of the other strip.

Eccentric coiling

In eccentric coils, the centre of the coil is pulled out to one side of the shape. They are often used for the bodies of animals or party balloons.

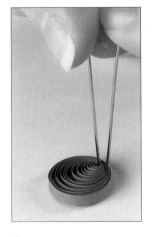

1 Form a basic closed coil. Insert a tall pin in the quilling board and place the coil next to it. Insert a second pin in the centre of the coil.

2 Pull the second pin towards the first, drawing the centre of the coil to one side.

3 Apply glue at the base of the eccentric coil (where the coils are closest together).

4 When the glue is dry, remove the pins.

Filigree quilling

Filigree quilling is a more delicate style of quilling in which the coils are not glued into a basic closed coil. Shapes are formed by first folding a paper strip in half and then coiling the end of the strip with a quilling tool and releasing it. I find it best to coil down to the fold or crease in the paper strip before removing the tool, and then teasing out the coil to the required length. When attaching filigree coils to a background, make sure the glue is applied to every part of the shape.

Heart

Hearts are usually made using a ¼ strip.

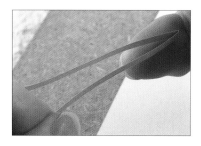

1 Fold the paper strip in half and crease it at the bottom.

2 Coil one side of the paper strip inwards, towards the centre of the 'V', using a quilling tool.

3 Remove the quilling tool, and coil the other side of the paper strip inwards, to the same depth.

A completed heart.

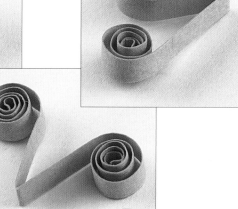

'V' coil

Made in the same way as a heart, but with the coils formed outwards.

Scroll

Both coils are formed in the same direction, one higher than the other.

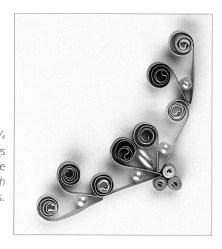

I have made this corner filigree from four ¼ strip scroll shapes and three ⅛ strip pegs in graduated purple and pink papers. Once glued down, I decorated the motif with 3mm pearl beads.

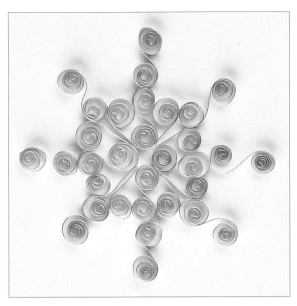

This delicate silver snowflake is made of ¼ strip 'S' and 'V' coils using silver-edged white paper. There is a template for this shape on page 46.

'S' coil

1 Find the central point of the paper strip by folding it in half, but do not crease it.

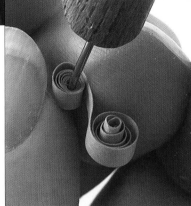

2 Coil both ends of the paper down to the centre to form an 'S' shape.

'P' coil

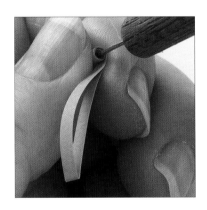

A completed 'P' coil.

Fold the paper strip in half, crease it, and coil both ends together using a quilling tool, working towards the fold. The strip forming the inner coil will bend away from the other as you work.

This flamboyant bird has a teardrop-shape body made from two strips joined together in parallel, a ¼ strip teardrop head and a ½ strip leaf-shape neck. The rest of the motif is made from various filigree shapes, and decorated with pearl beads.

Wheatears (single looping)

These are very useful shapes, formed without the quilling tool, which can be made any size and shaped with the fingers. Always start with a full-length strip of paper and trim off any excess when you have made the required number of loops.

1 Make a loop at one end of the paper strip.

2 Apply glue along the edge of the paper.

3 Glue the ends of the loop together, then start to wrap the paper around the loop to form the second loop.

4 Apply glue to the base of the second loop.

5 Continue making loops in the paper, applying glue at the base of each loop before moving on to the next. When you have made the desired number of loops, cut off the paper strip just below the base, fold over the excess paper and glue it in position.

The completed loops.

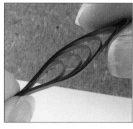

This shape is formed by pinching the base and gently squeezing the loops as you slide your fingers up the shape and pinch the top, forming an elongated leaf shape.

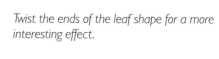

For a wing or petal shape, form a leaf shape, then push the tips back towards each other.

Twist the ends of the leaf shape for a more interesting effect.

Quilled roses

Quilled roses can be made with any width of paper, but for more delicate ones use 3mm wide strips. Roses look especially realistic when made with graduated papers, but there is plenty of scope to use your imagination and experiment with different colours. Use green paper strips to make cabbages and lettuces!

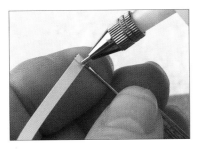

1 Form the centre of the rose by turning the paper strip once around the quilling tool and gluing it in place.

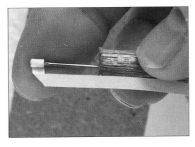

2 Fold the paper down towards the handle of the quilling tool, forming an accurate right angle.

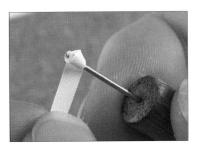

3 Roll the paper strip loosely over the fold so that you don't crush the rose shape as it forms. Continue rolling until the paper is at right angles to the quilling tool.

4 Continue folding and coiling, holding the petals in place with your forefinger as you work.

5 As you fold and coil, make sure the rose shape is tight at the base and fans out towards the top.

6 When your rose is the desired size, remove the quilling tool. The coils will unwind slightly, and the rose will open out.

7 Trim off the excess paper using a diagonal cut, add a dab of glue to the end of the paper and secure it on the back of the rose.

A completed rose.

Making borders and motifs

When making a motif, first quill all the shapes required. More complicated designs will need a template, which can be protected from glue by covering it with either greaseproof or tracing paper. Secure your shapes on a quilling board using pins to stop them moving around, and glue them together. Apply glue to the sides of the shapes so that the completed motif does not become stuck to the board and can be lifted off easily. Compare your motif on various backgrounds before deciding on which one to use, and then glue it in place.

Borders are usually composed of different elements. Make each element separately, then arrange them on your background before gluing them down. Always start at the centre of the border and work outwards to ensure the shapes are evenly spaced.

You will need

For the candle motif:

5 x ½ strip red pegs

1 x ⅛ strip yellow teardrop

1 x ¼ strip cream scroll

3 x ¼ strip gold-edged green holly-leaf shapes

3 x ⅛ strip red pegs

Quilling board

Scrap sheet of white paper

4 drawing pins

Selection of long and short round-headed pins

Copy of the template

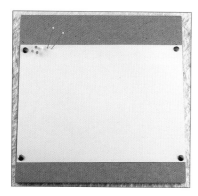

1 Begin by preparing your work surface. Pin a sheet of paper on to your quilling board. Keep some pins handy for holding your quilled shapes in place as you work.

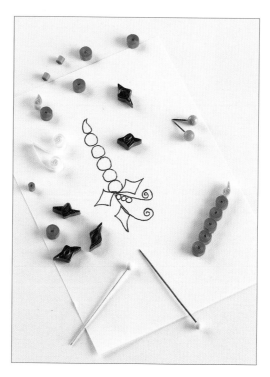

2 Gather together everything you need to make the motif or border, including the quilled shapes, template and pins.

Template for the motif (reproduced actual size).

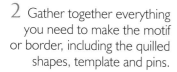

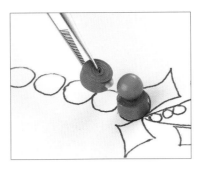

3 Pin the template to the board, and pin on the peg at the base of the candle using a round-headed pin. Position the peg so that the join will be hidden by the second peg.

4 Put a dab of glue on a second peg so that it covers the join, and attach it to the first.

5 Complete the candle following this method, finishing with the flame at the top. Use as many pins as you need.

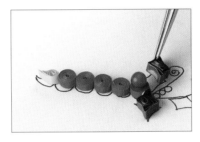

6 Arrange two leaves and the filigree at the base of the candle. Make sure you are happy with the arrangement before gluing them down.

7 Glue the two leaves in place, applying the glue to the sides of the leaves where they touch the candle.

8 Put a dab of glue along the folded edge of the filigree shape and attach it to the leaves. Attach the remaining elements in the same way.

9 When dry, remove the pin and lift the completed motif off the template, loosening it first with the tip of a round-ended knife if necessary.

10 Apply glue to the back of the motif, making sure you cover every element. You can also do this by dipping a cocktail stick in glue and rolling it back and forth across the back of the motif.

11 Attach the motif to your chosen background.

Imagine a themed Christmas table with the place cards and napkin holders decorated with quilled motifs, or coordinating gift tags, gift boxes, Christmas cards and tree decorations. The photograph opposite shows just some of the ways you can use quilled designs to create a themed 'look' for Christmas. Extend this idea to other celebrations to make them extra special, such as birthdays, anniversaries and weddings.

Using borders and motifs

You can use borders and motifs as accents to enhance larger quilled projects, or they can be mounted to form the main subject of a greetings card, gift tag, place card or picture frame. On these two pages are some ideas for laying out borders and motifs. Most of them can be adapted to suit any size or style of background, so simply use your imagination and have fun!

Roses create a perfect border around an aperture card, either going part of the way round (as shown above), or encircling it completely.

Many of the motifs in this book can be extended to form a long border down the side of a card, for example by adding the line of leaves above and below this owl motif.

Small motifs at opposite corners of a card create a delicate look for a wedding invitation, greetings card or place card.

Placing small motifs at opposite corners that echo the main design in the centre of a card can be very effective.

Filigree borders can be used along two sides of a card or frame, or extended to go all the way round the edge.

A motif or border placed in a corner and extending part of the way round two sides of a card looks very effective, especially when echoed by a smaller version in the opposite corner.

Four tiny, themed motifs placed in the corners of a card can be used to border an invitation or thank-you card, or a larger quilled motif in the centre of a greetings card.

These quilled motifs follow the curve of an oval aperture. This design could be repeated in the opposite corner.

Individual quilled motifs can be placed in a line along the bottom edge of a landscape card to form an interesting and lively border.

Flowers

Quilling flowers is a joy, as such a huge range of colours and forms can be used and combined. Recreate real flowers from nature, or design complete fantasy flowers in which any combination of colours can be used.

Daisy motif

The daisy centre is a ¼ strip yellow peg and the seven petals are ⅓ strip white marquises. The leaves are six ½ strip green marquises and a ¼ strip green scroll. This design is decorated with 3mm pearl beads. (See template on page 44.)

Blue fantasy flower

This flower is made with three ⅛ strip pegs (two turquoise and one deep blue), two ½ strip deep blue leaf shapes, two ¼ strip pale blue leaf shapes, a ¼ strip turquoise teardrop and a ¼ strip turquoise scroll. It is finished with four 3mm pearl beads. (See template on page 44.)

Yellow fantasy flower

Two ½ strip orange leaf shapes, two ¼ strip pale yellow leaf shapes, a ¼ strip central dark yellow teardrop and a ¼ strip pale green scroll have been used to make this flower. It is decorated with 3mm pearl beads and elongated pearl beads. (See template on page 44.)

Pink and green fantasy flower

The pink and green fantasy flower has two ½ strip pale green leaf shapes, a ¼ strip pink teardrop in the centre and two ¼ strip 'V' shape filigree scrolls. Pearl beads are used for decoration. (See template on page 44.)

Lilac fantasy flower

The lilac fantasy flower has four ½ strip leaf shapes in shades of lilac, and a ¼ strip pale green scroll. It is decorated with round and elongated pearl beads. (See template on page 44.)

Daisy border

The small blue flowers are made of five ⅛ strip blue pegs around a ⅛ strip yellow peg centre. The daisies have ¼ strip yellow peg centres, with seven ⅛ strip white marquises for petals. The connecting pale yellow leaf shapes are ⅛ and ¼ strips.

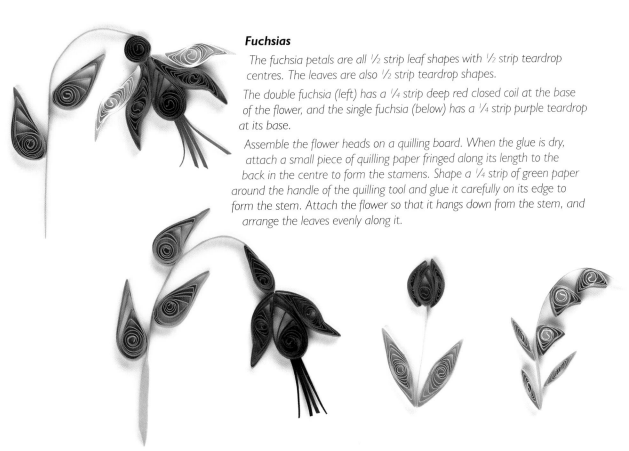

Fuchsias

The fuchsia petals are all ½ strip leaf shapes with ½ strip teardrop centres. The leaves are also ½ strip teardrop shapes.

The double fuchsia (left) has a ¼ strip deep red closed coil at the base of the flower, and the single fuchsia (below) has a ¼ strip purple teardrop at its base.

Assemble the flower heads on a quilling board. When the glue is dry, attach a small piece of quilling paper fringed along its length to the back in the centre to form the stamens. Shape a ¼ strip of green paper around the handle of the quilling tool and glue it carefully on its edge to form the stem. Attach the flower so that it hangs down from the stem, and arrange the leaves evenly along it.

Daffodils

Daffodil leaves can be made from either wheatears (the number of loops varied to make different lengths of leaf) or full-strip leaf shapes. Each stem is made from a ¼ strip of green paper, coiled at one end for a quarter of its length and glued into a teardrop shape. The rest of the strip becomes the stem, which can be trimmed to the required length.

The petals of the left-hand flower are four ¼ strip yellow leaf shapes with a ¼ strip deep yellow holly-leaf shape centre. The central daffodil has ¼ strip leaf-shape petals and an orange ¼ strip holly-leaf shape centre. Each flower head of the daffodil clump on the right is made of two ¼ strip yellow teardrops with a ¼ strip pale yellow half-moon centre.

Roses

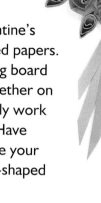

Roses make beautiful designs, especially for romantic celebrations such as anniversaries, weddings and Valentine's Day. They look particularly effective when made using graduated papers.

Designs that include roses should first be laid out on a quilling board to ensure the elements are positioned correctly, then glued together on your chosen background. Start with the main roses and gradually work outwards, incorporating any leaves, scrolls or other elements. Have fun combining different-coloured roses and leaves, and decorate your creations with beads and pegs. Leaves can be marquise- or leaf-shaped and made using ¼ or ⅛ strips.

Rose bouquet

Draw a faint circle, the size of an eggcup, on to the card. Fill this shape with roses, covering the pencil marks. Arrange a ¼ strip green scroll and two ⅛ strips folded in half to make ribbons hanging down from the base of the bouquet. Place nine ⅛ strip green teardrop-shape leaves evenly around the outside of the bouquet.

White rose motif

Glue three roses to the card, a ¼ strip 'V' coil which has one end longer than the other, four ½ strip leaves and 3mm pearl bead decorations.

Rose trellis

Glue a trellis of beige papers flat on the card using two uprights placed 1cm (½in) apart, one 13cm (5in) long and the other 10cm (4in) long. Attach two cross bars, 3cm (1½in) long, diagonally across at the top and the bottom.

Make a selection of nine roses, sixteen ⅛ strip teardrop leaves and tendrils made from ⅛ strips coiled along half their length. Assemble the design from the base upwards.

Red rose corner spray

This border can be used around any shaped aperture or the corner of a card. Try starting with a deep colour and make the roses progressively paler. Build up the design starting at one end, placing two ¼ strip marquise leaves between each rose.

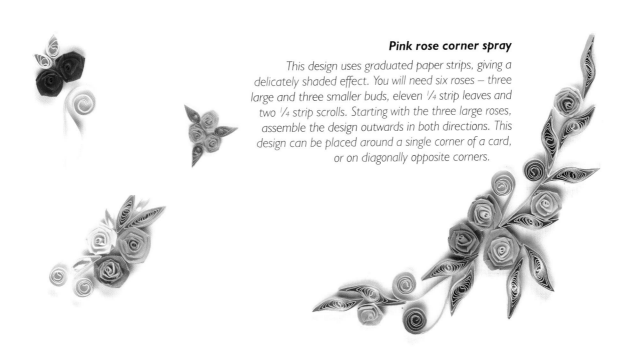

Pink rose corner spray

This design uses graduated paper strips, giving a delicately shaded effect. You will need six roses – three large and three smaller buds, eleven $1/4$ strip leaves and two $1/4$ strip scrolls. Starting with the three large roses, assemble the design outwards in both directions. This design can be placed around a single corner of a card, or on diagonally opposite corners.

Rose garland

Draw lightly around a small cup with an embossing tool to mark the card. Make nine roses in different shades of pink and four deep red roses. Quill nine $1/4$ strip 'S' coils, seven $1/4$ strip leaves and two $1/4$ strip scrolls using green paper. Arrange the scrolls and roses evenly around the circle, starting at its base, leaving a gap just off-centre at the top and bottom of the design. Place scrolls, roses and leaves in these gaps to form motifs at the top and bottom of the garland. Adjust the number of roses and leaves if necessary.

Pink rose corner motif

This motif is quilled using graduated papers and decorated with 3mm pearl beads. The leaves and scroll are all made with $1/4$ strips.

The Pond

Imagine a country pond on a summer's day, teeming with life – dragonflies hovering above it, ducks swimming and diving for food, colourful irises growing on its banks, frogs hiding under rocks and in the undergrowth, not to mention the fish swimming in the water itself. The picture I've just painted gave me inspiration for the motifs and borders on this page, which could be combined to create a whole pond-life scene.

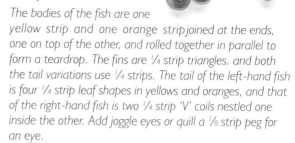

Goldfish

The bodies of the fish are one yellow strip and one orange strip joined at the ends, one on top of the other, and rolled together in parallel to form a teardrop. The fins are 1/4 strip triangles. and both the tail variations use 1/4 strips. The tail of the left-hand fish is four 1/4 strip leaf shapes in yellows and oranges, and that of the right-hand fish is two 1/4 strip 'V' coils nestled one inside the other. Add joggle eyes or quill a 1/8 strip peg for an eye.

You can achieve some wonderful effects by using different shades of paper quilled in parallel for the bodies, or perhaps use more exotic colours and designs to quill a selection of tropical fish!

Frog border

Frogs are great fun – you can change their characters by the twist of the mouth or the set of their eyes! The larger frog on the left has a body of one full-strip green eccentric coil, two upper legs of 1/2 strip teardrops and two lower legs of 1/4 strip teardrops. The mouth is a yellow 1/2 strip joined in series with a green 1/2 strip, coiled into a leaf shape starting with the yellow. Each eye is a black 1/4 strip joined in series with a yellow 1/4 strip and a green 1/4 strip, coiled into a peg starting with the black. The smaller frogs are made in the same way, but with no upper legs and all the dimensions halved. Give them either a leaf-shape mouth or a marquise-shape mouth. To assemble the frogs, start by pinning down the mouth and build the rest of the design around it.

The bulrushes are wheatear leaves of varying lengths with stems cut to length and glued on their edges. The flower heads are 1/4 strip leaf shapes, as is the water. To finish, add butterfly stickers, or quill your own butterflies following the instructions on pages 30–31.

Templates are provided for the frogs on page 45.

Ducks border

These playful ducks are all quilled in the same way, but the shapes are positioned differently on the $\frac{1}{2}$ and $\frac{1}{4}$ strip leaf shapes which form the water. The ducks' bodies are $\frac{1}{2}$ strip teardrops and their heads are $\frac{1}{4}$ strip closed coils. Pull the heads into a size that is in proportion to the bodies. Complete the ducks with $\frac{1}{4}$ strip teardrop wings, $\frac{1}{8}$ strip triangular feet, and a $\frac{1}{16}$ strip teardrop beak. Assemble the ducks on a quilling board, gluing the wings on top of the body if possible to give a three-dimensional effect.

Tadpoles

Add these fun accents to the inside of a card or swimming along a gift tag with a pond-life theme! They are very simple to quill – just $\frac{1}{4}$ strips coiled almost to the end and then glued and shaped into a teardrop leaving a small tag for the tail.

Golden iris

The leaves are marquises (four $\frac{3}{4}$ strip and one $\frac{1}{2}$ strip) quilled using graduated papers. The flower head, starting at the top, consists of two mid-yellow $\frac{1}{2}$ strip teardrops, two light yellow $\frac{1}{4}$ strip leaf shapes, two mid-yellow $\frac{1}{2}$ strip half moons and a central dark yellow $\frac{1}{2}$ strip teardrop. (See template on page 45.)

Dragonfly motif

I have used vibrant blues and turquoises for the dragonfly's body and silver-edged white paper for its wings. Assemble the head and body first, starting with the head. The head is a turquoise $\frac{1}{2}$ strip joined in series with a deep blue $\frac{1}{2}$ strip, coiled into a peg starting with the turquoise. Next are two pegs made in the same way with $\frac{1}{4}$ strips. The two pegs after that are $\frac{1}{4}$ strip turquoise, and the next two are $\frac{1}{4}$ strip dark blue. Lastly are two $\frac{1}{8}$ turquoise strips and a $\frac{1}{8}$ deep blue teardrop.

Both pairs of wings are wheatears, made long and pointed, with six loops for the top wings and five loops for the bottom wings.

Kissing ducks

These ducks make cute anniversary or Valentine's Day cards, or fun place cards for a wedding. Either make the ducks to the same dimensions as those in the border at the top of the page, or use $\frac{1}{4}$ strips for the bodies, $\frac{1}{8}$ strips for the heads and $\frac{1}{16}$ strips for the beaks. Add silver heart stickers to complete the design.

Butterflies

I enjoy quilling butterflies as I can really use my imagination and invent exciting colour combinations, wing and body shapes! All the different parts of the butterflies on these pages are interchangeable, and I hope you will experiment and create your own varieties of butterfly.

To make a wheatear wing, start with a complete paper strip and trim it once the wing is the required size. Leave it rounded, or shape it following the directions on page 16. The antennae are formed using either a scroll or a 'V' coil, or alternatively leave a 1 or 2cm (½ or ¾in) tag uncoiled when forming the head, glue the head shape together, then cut the excess paper in half lengthways and coil each half into a scroll or a 'V' shape.

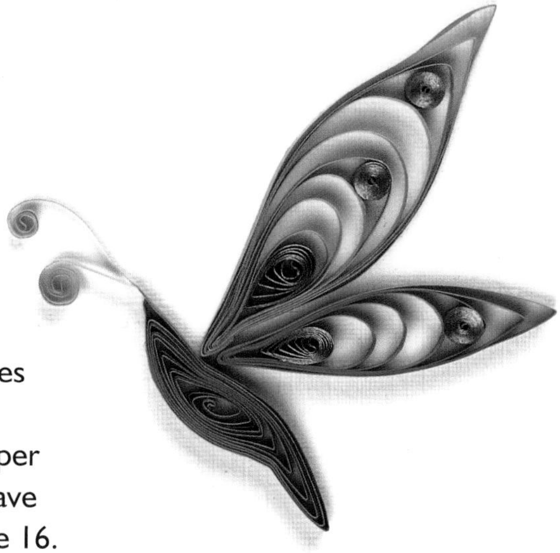

Jade and turquoise butterfly

The body is one turquoise strip and one jade strip joined in parallel and coiled into a leaf shape. The wing decorations are ¼ strip pegs and ¼ strip teardrops.

Three-wing butterfly

The body is a full-strip leaf shape, and the wing decorations are ½ strip teardrops and pearl beads.

Green butterfly

The body is a full-strip teardrop, and the head is a ¼ strip closed coil. The wing decorations are ⅛ strip pegs and ¼ strip teardrops.

Peach butterfly

This delicate butterfly has three-looped wheatear top wings and ¼ strip teardrop bottom wings. The head is a ⅛ strip peg and the body is a ½ strip marquise, both of which are made from gold-edged paper. The flower spray has a ⅛ strip peg in the centre, and ⅛ strip teardrop petals and buds. The leaves are ¼ strip marquises. (See template on page 45.)

Pink and purple graduated butterfly

This butterfly is made using graduated papers. The top wings are ½ strip leaf shapes and the bottom wings are ⅓ strip teardrops. The body is a ½ strip marquise and the head is a ¼ strip peg.

Pointed-winged butterfly

The head is a ½ strip peg and the body consists of two ½ strip pegs, three ¼ strip pegs and two ⅛ strip pegs. Coloured seed beads have been used to decorate the wings.

Blue and silver butterfly

The body of this butterfly is a ½ strip teardrop made from silver-edged white paper, which is also used for the 'P' coil antennae. The top wings are ½ strip silver-edged white paper joined in series with ½ strip blue paper coiled into a teardrop shape, starting with the white. The bottom wings are ½ strip teardrops.

Pink butterfly

The body is a full-strip leaf shape. The wheatear wings are decorated with pearl beads.

Butterfly border

All these butterflies are made from graduated papers and have ⅓ strip top wings and ¼ strip bottom wings. The bodies are ⅓ strip marquises, and the wing shapes are either marquises or teardrops. The linking flowers are ⅛ pegs with ¼ strip marquise leaves.

Yellow butterfly

The head is a ¼ strip teardrop and the body is a ½ strip teardrop. Pearl beads are used to decorate the wings.

Christmas

Christmas motifs can be used in so many different ways, from cards and gift tags to tree and cake decorations. Try different colour schemes from the traditional green and red, such as blue and silver or white and gold.

Jingle bells border

First make three bells, each from one strip of paper. You also need six ¼ strip holly-leaf shapes and six ¼ strip scrolls made from gold-edged green papers. Decorate with gold and red 3mm beads after the design has been attached to the card. (See template on page 46.)

Blue and gold candle

This unusual colour combination also works well in more traditional red and green. The candle needs five ½ strip gold-edged blue pegs, though the length of the candle can be extended by using more pegs. The flame is a ¼ strip gold-edged white teardrop, the six holly leaves are each made from a ¼ gold-edged white strip, and there are two gold-edged blue scrolls and 3mm pearl beads to decorate.

Keep the candle straight on the quilling board by ruling on a pencil line as a guide. (See template on page 45.)

White Christmas tree

This tree is made with ten ½ strip teardrops using white, gold-edged paper. Three ⅛ strip teardrops and six ⅛ strip pegs are used for the decorations. The pot is one full-strip square shape and the star a ¼ strip holly shape.

Assemble this design from the base of the tree upwards, keeping the shape as symmetrical as possible. Glue on the decorations while the tree is still on the quilling board.

A smaller tree can be quilled using only three teardrops and a ¼ strip pot.

Christmas garland

This garland is made from ¼ strip holly shapes in two shades of green, gold-edged green and gold-edged cream, approximately five shapes in each colour, depending on the size of the garland. Draw a faint circle on your card and glue the holly shapes at varying angles around it, making sure you cover the pencil mark. Decorate the garland with a bow made from a long strip of red paper, and decorate it with red and gold seed beads.

Poinsettia

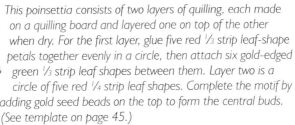

This poinsettia consists of two layers of quilling, each made on a quilling board and layered one on top of the other when dry. For the first layer, glue five red $^1/_3$ strip leaf-shape petals together evenly in a circle, then attach six gold-edged green $^1/_3$ strip leaf shapes between them. Layer two is a circle of five red $^1/_4$ strip leaf shapes. Complete the motif by adding gold seed beads on the top to form the central buds. (See template on page 45.)

Robin

This cheeky little robin can be repeated along the edge of a card to form a border or used as a single motif. The body is a $^1/_2$ strip teardrop, the tail a $^1/_4$ strip indented triangle and the head a $^1/_4$ strip closed coil. The robin's red breast is a $^1/_2$ strip half-moon shape, pinned closely to the body on a quilling board until the glue is dry. The legs are $^1/_8$ strip marquises and the tiny beak is a $^1/_{16}$ strip marquise. Decorate with two $^1/_4$ strip holly leaves, a $^1/_4$ strip scroll and red seed bead berries. (See template on page 46.)

Angels border

The stars, wings and halos are all quilled with gold-edged cream paper strips, the bodies and heads are white and the feet palest pink. $^1/_4$ strip holly-leaf shapes are used for the linking stars, and each angel has a $^1/_2$ strip triangular body with a $^1/_4$ strip closed coil head pulled into a size that is in proportion to the body. The wings are $^1/_4$ strip teardrops, the halos $^1/_8$ strip marquises and the feet $^1/_8$ strip pegs.

Gold candles and holly border

This border can be extended with extra scrolls and holly. First make the two candles on the quilling board, one with five and one with four pegs and each made of $^1/_2$ strip gold-edged paper. The flames are $^1/_4$ strip leaf shapes. Quill the rest of the shapes – four deep red roses, three cream roses, nine $^1/_2$ strip gold-edged green holly leaves, two scrolls and two 'V' coils in gold-edged cream paper – then arrange the design on the quilling board without gluing before attaching it to your chosen background.

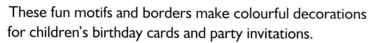

Flying High!

These fun motifs and borders make colourful decorations for children's birthday cards and party invitations.

Kite motif

Children's kites can be many different colours and the tail can be extended to form a colourful border. For this kite you will need two $\frac{1}{2}$ strip triangles (one red and one orange), two full-strip triangles in the same colours and two $\frac{1}{4}$ strip yellow triangles. The tail is made from six $\frac{1}{4}$ strip triangles attached in pairs either side of a 10cm (4in) long paper strip glued along its edge. (See template on page 46.)

Party balloon border

All the balloons in this border are $\frac{1}{2}$ strip closed coils with a 1 or 2cm ($\frac{1}{2}$ or $\frac{3}{4}$in) tag left uncoiled for the string. The musical notes are $\frac{1}{8}$ strip pegs with a short tag left uncoiled. Arrange the shapes at varying angles on the card, and finish by decorating with star stickers.

Bird of paradise

The bird's body is a full-strip teardrop shape, its head is a $\frac{1}{4}$ strip teardrop and the beak is a $\frac{1}{16}$ strip teardrop. Both wings are formed from three $\frac{1}{4}$ strip scrolls, and the tail is a $\frac{1}{4}$ strip 'V' coil and two $\frac{1}{4}$ strip 'P' coils. I have used different blues throughout and 3mm beads for the eye and decorations. I have deliberately glued the beads with their holes uppermost for an unusual effect. (See template on page 46.)

Bunch of balloons

These balloons can be used for birthday cards or children's party invitations. Quill the same number of balloons as the child's age, or spell out their name on the balloons with alphabet stickers. Each balloon is a full-strip eccentric coil with a ¼ strip triangle for the knot at its base.

Hot-air balloon border

Make the balloons progressively smaller towards the top of the border to suggest perspective and distance. Each balloon is a wheatear made using two colours joined in parallel. Make each loop with both strips together, then loosen the outer strip to make a larger loop. The baskets are either full-strip or ½ strip squares, depending on the balloon's size. The tiny birds are all made from two ⅛ strip leaf shapes joined at an angle.

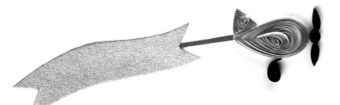

Sky banner

The banner behind the aeroplane can be extended to accommodate any length of message – perhaps the person's name, age or a greeting such as 'Happy Birthday'. The plane's body is a full-strip teardrop made using silver-edged white paper, the wing is a ¼ strip teardrop and the tail fin a ¼ strip triangle. The propeller is a ⅛ strip peg plus two ⅛ strip marquises, and the wheel is a ⅛ strip that has been coiled leaving a short tag.

The Sky

The theme of these two pages includes spaceships, fireworks, suns, moons and stars – all suitable for children's party invitations (particularly bonfire parties) and greetings cards. These designs work very well with metallic-edged papers, and can be made more dramatic by placing them on dark-coloured backgrounds.

Spaceship

This fun spaceship is made with silver-edged white paper and has black antennae and yellow windows. The body is made from a full-strip marquise and a ½ strip half moon. Each of the three legs is a ⅛ strip marquise and a ⅛ strip peg.

The three windows are ⅛ strip pegs glued on to the main body of the spaceship, and the antennae are ⅛ pegs with a small tag left uncoiled.

Rocket

The body of the rocket is quilled from metallic-edged red and green papers. The central part is a full-strip green rectangle, the nose cone is a ½ strip red triangle and the base is a ½ strip red square. Glue a paper strip 3cm (1 ¼in) long behind the rocket and arrange eight ⅛ strip marquises along it in red, yellow and orange.

Moons and stars border

This border looks particularly good on a deep blue background with white silver-edged stars. Try placing it around an oval aperture. I have used ¼ strip gold-edged cream paper quilled into a holly-leaf shape for the stars, and then added extra small sticker stars. The moons are ½ strip half-moon shapes.

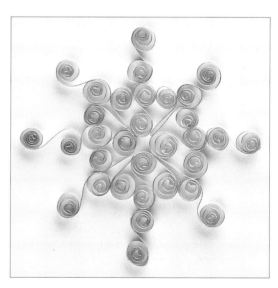

Silver snowflake

This delicate silver snowflake is made of ¼ strip 'S' and 'V' coils using silver-edged white paper. (See template on page 46.)

Sun

Use different reds, oranges and yellows for this sun, or alternatively make it using a single colour. The sun itself is a full-strip eccentric coil. The rays are formed using six orange ⅓ strip leaf shapes spaced evenly around the centre, and nine ¼ strip leaf shapes in shades of yellow placed randomly between them.

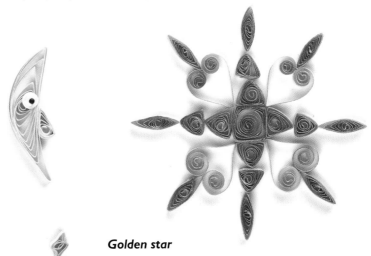

Filigree cloud

Clouds can be made any shape or size. I have used ¼ strip scrolls for this cloud, placed randomly on the background. Fill any awkward spaces using ⅛ strip closed coils. The birds are ¼ strip leaf shapes and ⅛ strip pegs.

Angel

This angel also works well quilled all in white, and the same design could be used to make a fairy. The angel's skirt is four wheatears, each with four loops, between which are ¼ strip teardrops. Her body is a ½ strip teardrop, her face a full-strip closed coil (pulled to size), and her hair ⅛ strip 'S' coils. Her wings each consist of a ½ strip teardrop and a ¼ strip teardrop. (See template on page 47.)

The Plough

I have arranged these stars, each a ⅛ strip holly leaf, in the shape of the constellation The Plough.

Golden star

This star is made from gold-edged cream paper, and is also effective in pale yellow or gold-edged white paper. In the centre is a ½ strip square shape and around this are eight triangles, four hearts and eight marquises, all ¼ strip. Keep this star symmetrical by constructing it on a sheet of graph paper, or use two rules placed at right angles to each other as a guide. (See template on page 47.)

Weddings

A wedding day is very special, and what could be more wonderful than to quill coordinating invitations, orders of service, place cards and menus. Enhance the wedding photographs by quilling a border around the frame, or create a memory box for all the wedding momentoes. A quilled card sent to the bride and groom will be treasured for always.

Lucky horseshoe

I have decorated this horseshoe using roses in various shades of pink with 1/8 teardrop shapes for the leaves.

Match the colour of the roses to the bridesmaids' dresses or to the general theme of the wedding. (Use this picture as a template for the horseshoe shape.)

Champagne glasses

I made these using white silver-edged paper strips. The line of bubbles could be extended to form a border. For each glass use a full-strip triangle and two 1/4 strip marquises. For the bubbles use 1/8 strip pegs and 3mm pearl beads.

Wedding rings

The two wedding rings would work well as a central motif, with the flowers extending either side. I have used one strip of gold-edged paper for the rings, coiled around a thick pen. The roses are made using graduated paper, and the leaves are each 1/8 strip teardrops. Assemble the design on your card or other background by first gluing the rings in the centre, followed by the roses, and then arranging the leaves in between.

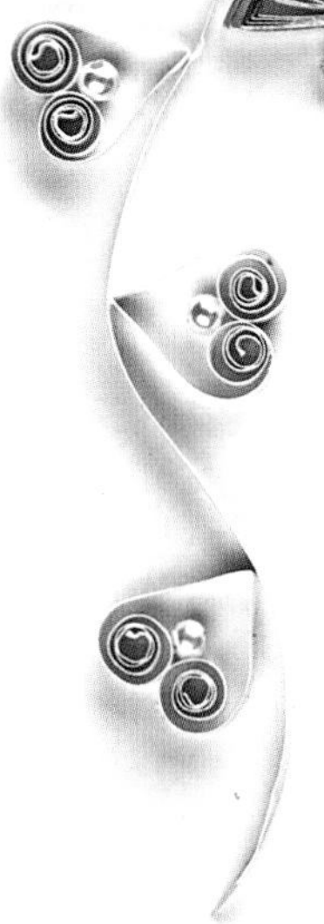

Bells and hearts

This border and motif could be extended to fit any size background. The two bells are each made using a full-length strip, and the two scrolls and the hearts each consist of ¼ strips. The two tendrils are each 90mm (3½in) long, and glued down along one edge. The finished design is decorated with 3mm pearl beads.

Bride

The bride's skirt is made from three wheatears, each with six loops, and two ¼ strip teardrops placed between them. Her body is a ½ strip teardrop. Her hat consists of a ½ strip leaf shape for the brim; a ¼ strip half moon for the crown (shaped to fit) and a ¼ strip scroll for the ribbon. The flowers in her bouquet are ¹⁄₁₆ strip pegs and the leaves ¹⁄₁₆ strip teardrops. (See template on page 47.)

Ribbon and roses border

The bow at the top of this border is made from two ½ strip and two ¼ strip teardrops and a ¼ strip 'V' coil. Glue a length of quilling paper flat on the card and attach groups of roses at regular intervals along it. The ⅛ strip leaves and the ¼ strip scroll are added at the end to complete the design.

Dove

This delicate motif would work well on place cards. For the dove use a ½ strip teardrop for the body; a ½ strip triangle for the tail; a ½ strip closed coil for the head (pulled to size); a ⅛ strip teardrop for the beak; and a ½ strip teardrop for each wing. The two hearts are ¼ strip filigrees.

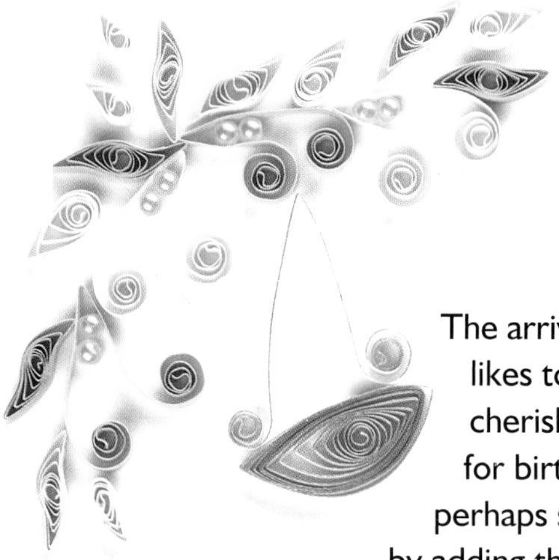

Babies

The arrival of a new baby is so special that everyone likes to send a card that the proud parents can cherish for always. These borders and motifs are suitable for birth and Christening cards, birth announcements or perhaps scrapbook pages of the new baby. Personalise the card by adding the baby's name and birth date using stickers.

Cradle in the flowers

The flower spray is made from four ¼ strip scrolls and seven ¼ strip leaves, all in two shades of green. The flower buds consist of three ¼ strip and three ⅛ strip teardrops in white. It is decorated with 3mm pearl beads. The cradle is a full-strip half moon in silver-edged white paper with a ½ strip 'V' coil handle. (See template on page 47.)

Blue pram

The body of the pram consists of 1 ½ strips joined in series and quilled into a half moon, and the hood is a full-strip half moon. The wheels are ½ strip closed coils supported on a ¼ strip 'S' coil, and the handle is a ¼ strip scroll. The hood is decorated with ⅛ pegs alternating with 3mm blue beads.

Stork and baby

For the stork I have used a full-strip teardrop for the body, a ¼ strip teardrop for the head, and a ¼ strip triangle for the beak. Use a ¼ strip coiled halfway along its length and glued into a teardrop for the legs and feet. The eye is a ⅛ strip peg. The baby consists of a ¼ strip closed coil head, and a ½ strip teardrop and two ¼ strip teardrops shaped around each other for the shawl.

Baby's bonnet

This simple motif is a full-strip half moon with a ribbon glued on to one corner. The flower is made from ⅛ strip pegs.

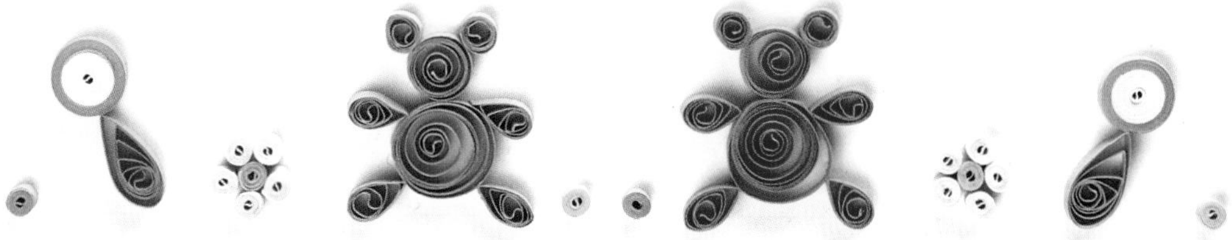

Teddy bear border

Each of the teddies has a ½ strip closed coil body, a ¼ strip closed coil head, ⅛ strip closed coil ears and ⅛ strip teardrop arms and legs. The rattles have ¼ strip teardrop handles, and a peg consisting of a white ¼ strip and a pink ¼ strip joined in series. The flowers and connecting pegs are all made from ⅛ strips. Any simple motifs could be incorporated into this border, perhaps using various shades of pink for a girl and blues for a boy.

Stork and crib

This stork flying in with the baby consists of two wings made from full-strip leaf shapes, a ½ strip teardrop head and a ¼ strip leaf-shape beak. The legs are made from a ½ strip folded in half, and each end coiled along half its length and glued into a teardrop. The baby basket is a ½ strip half-moon shape with a 'V' coil handle.

Pink crib

The body of the crib is 1 ½ strips joined in series and quilled into a half moon. The hood is a full-strip half moon decorated with two ⅛ strip 'S' coils, the legs are a ¼ strip 'V' coil and the blanket a ½ strip marquise.

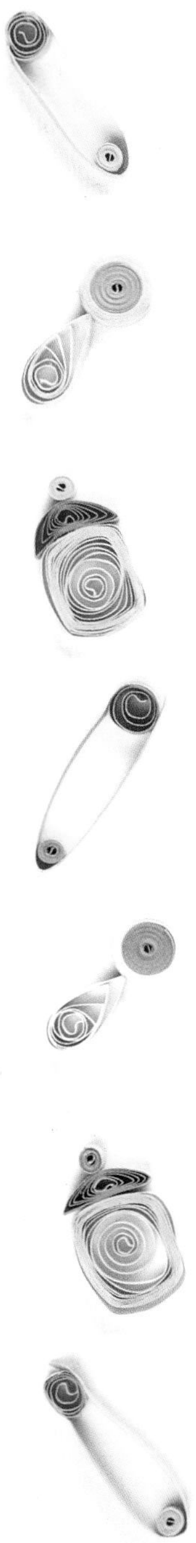

Baby border

Each of the elements in this border could also be used as individual motifs.

The safety pins are ¼ strips coiled halfway along their length, and then allowed to uncoil slightly and glued into a small closed coil. The rest of the strip is bent round to make a safety-pin shape and glued to the closed coil. A ⅛ strip peg is glued into the base of the pin.

The rattles are the same as those in the teddy bear border on the facing page, and the baby bottles are a full-strip rectangle, with a lid made from a ¼ strip half moon and a teat consisting of a ⅛ peg.

Mother and baby birds

The mother bird has a ½ strip teardrop body, a ¼ strip teardrop wing, a ¼ strip closed coil head (pulled to size) and a ⅛ strip teardrop beak. She is sitting on a ½ strip half-moon nest. The baby birds are each made from a ¼ strip teardrop body, a ⅛ strip teardrop wing, a ⅛ strip closed coil head and a ¹⁄₁₆ strip teardrop beak. The leaves are ¼ and ⅛ strip teardrops in various shades of green, and the buds are ⅛ strip teardrops.

When constructing the design, begin by assembling the birds on your quilling board, then glue down a length of green paper strip along its edge, then attach each of the elements, starting with the mother bird and working outwards.

Toys

Old-fashioned toys make us nostalgic for times gone by, and make wonderfully colourful decorations for children's greetings cards, party invitations and so on. The designs on these two pages can be tailored to the age of the child, for example by matching it to the number of carriages on the train or the number of yachts on the waves.

Jack-in-a-box

The jack-in-a-box can be quilled in as many different colours as you wish. Increase the length of his body, which consists of ½ strip squares, to make an unusual border. His arms are two ¼ strip leaf shapes and his head is a full-strip closed coil. His hat is made of three triangles – one ½ strip and two ¼ strips; the box is a full-strip red square; and the lid is a ⅓ strip marquise.

Toy rabbit

The rabbit's body is an eccentric coil consisting of a pink ½ strip joined in series with a white ½ strip. The tail is a ½ strip peg, the foot and arm are ¼ strip teardrops, and the head is a full-strip closed coil. The ears are marquises made from a pink ¼ strip joined in series with a white ¼ strip, with the tips bent over. For the balloon, make a full-strip eccentric coil and attach a ⅛ strip triangle at the base.

Toy mouse

All children love a pull-along toy, and this little mouse will be no exception! His body is a full-strip teardrop with a 2cm (¾in) tag left uncoiled for his tail. He has ⅛ strip pegs for both his nose and his eye. His ears are pink ⅛ strips joined in series to grey ⅛ strips and coiled into teardrops starting with the pink. The wheels are pegs made from black ⅛ strips joined in series with white ⅛ strips, coiled starting with the white. The string is a short length of paper strip glued along its edge.

Toy yachts

Each yacht has a hull made from a full-strip half moon and a ¼ strip leaf-shape flag. The sails consist of a ¾ strip and a ½ strip triangle. The waves are ⅓ strip scrolls made using graduated paper.

Toys and bricks

Each of the elements in this border, which I have arranged in a jumbled pile for a three-dimensional effect, could be used as separate motifs. The bricks, which are all ½ strip squares, are attached first, then the toys are glued on top.

The boat has ¼ strip triangular sails, a ⅛ strip teardrop flag and a ¼ strip marquise hull. The teddy bear has a ½ strip closed coil body and a ¼ strip closed coil head. His arms, legs and ears are all ⅛ strip teardrops, his ears then being shaped to fit around his head. The train and the carriage are ¼ strip squares, with wheels made of ¼ strip closed coils. The funnel is a ⅛ strip marquise.

Toy drum

This is made from two full-strip squares, with drumsticks consisting of ⅛ strips coiled into teardrops at one end. The musical notes are ⅛ strip pegs, with a tag left uncoiled and bent over at the end.

Doll

The doll's dress is a full-strip triangle and her head a 3 strip solid peg. Add in each strip after a few turns while coiling the peg by laying it over the end of the previous strip without gluing. Make the face more realistic by gently pushing the peg up into a dome shape. Strengthen the back of the head with a layer of PVA glue. The arms are ¼ strip pegs and the legs ¼ strip teardrops. Each plait is made from two ¼ strip teardrops with ⅛ strip triangles for bows. The top of her hair is a ½ strip teardrop. (See template on page 47.)

Toy train

The train can have as many carriages as you like. Perhaps spell out the child's name on the top of the carriages using sticker letters. The engine consists of four ½ strip squares with four ¼ strip closed coils for wheels. The funnel is a ¼ strip marquise, the boiler a ¼ strip half moon, and the smoke consists of ⅛ strip pegs. To assemble the engine, take a black ⅛ strip and coil a short length at each end into a peg. Leave a space in the centre long enough for the body and wheels. The carriages are two ½ strip squares with two ¼ strip closed coil wheels, and are assembled in the same way as the engine. The contents of each carriage are a mix of ⅛ strip pegs, ¼ strip pegs and ⅛ strip closed coils. The whole train is mounted on to a strip of paper glued flat on the background.

Templates

The templates on these pages are for the more complicated quilling designs shown on the preceding pages. They are all reproduced actual size. Designs that include roses need to be glued together on the finished card or other background, and so do not require a template.

Peacock's body (page 12).

Blue fantasy flower (page 24).

Yellow fantasy flower (page 24).

Lilac fantasy flower (page 24).

Pink and green fantasy flower (page 24).

Daisy motif (page 24).

Frog border (page 28).

Peach butterfly (page 30).

Golden iris (page 29).

Blue and gold candle (page 32).

Poinsettia (page 32).

Layer 1

Layer 2

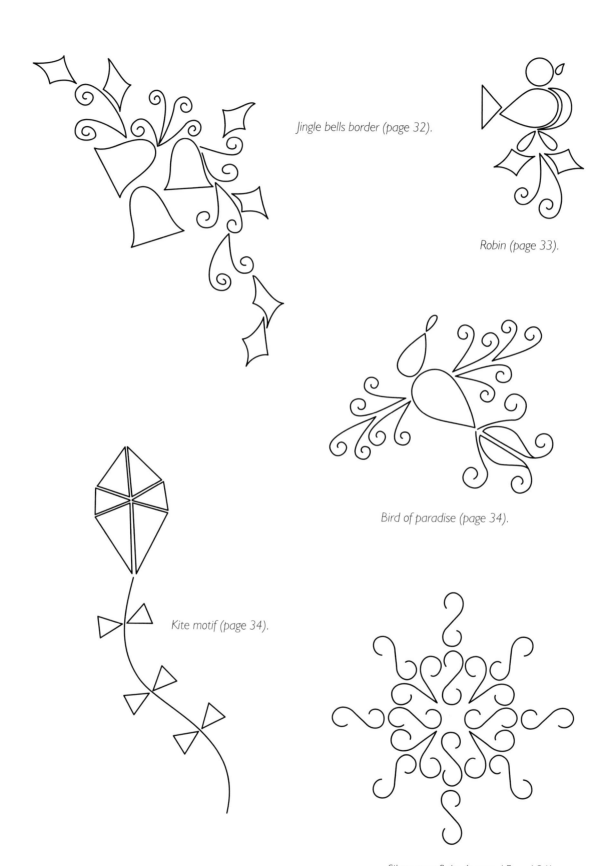

Jingle bells border (page 32).

Robin (page 33).

Bird of paradise (page 34).

Kite motif (page 34).

Silver snowflake (pages 15 and 36).

Golden star (page 37).

Angel (page 37).

Bouquet

Bride (page 39).

Doll (page 43).

Cradle in the flowers (page 40).

Index